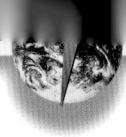

NATURE'S FURY

HURRICANE!

Anne Rooney

W
FRANKLIN WATTS
LONDON • SYDNEY

First published in 2006 by
Franklin Watts
338 Euston Road
London NW1 3BH

Franklin Watts Australia
Hachette Children's Books
Level 17/207 Kent St, Sydney, NSW 2000

Produced by Arcturus Publishing Limited,
26/27 Bickels Yard, 151–153 Bermondsey Street, London SE1 3HA

3233229

Editor: Alex Woolf
Design: www.mindseyedesign.co.uk
Consultant: Dr Andrew Coburn

Picture credits:
Corbis: 4 (Mike Theiss/Jim Reed Photography), 5 (Bettmann), 6 (Reuters), 8 (NASA),
9 (Eric Nguyen/Jim Reed Photography), 13 (David Tulis), 15 (Matthew Cavanaugh/EPA),
17 (Will and Deni McIntyre), 18 (NASA/JPL-Caltech), 19 (Rick Wilking/Reuters), 20
(Richard Carson/Reuters), 23 (Reuters), 24 (John Heseltine), 25 (Rafiqur Rahman/Reuters),
27 (Jim Edds/Jim Reed Photography), 28 (David J. Phillip/Pool/Reuters).
NASA Visible Earth: 11 (Jacques Descloitres, MODIS Rapid Response Team,
NASA/GSFC), 26 (Scott Dunbar, NASA JPL), 29.
Science Photo Library: 7 (NASA), 10 (NOAA), 12 (Carl Purcell), 14 (Mike Theiss/Jim Reed
Photography), 16 (Jim Reed).
TopFoto: 21, 22.

Anne Rooney asserts her moral right to be recognized as the
author of this work.
www.annerooney.co.uk

A CIP catalogue record for this book is available from the British Library

Dewey Decimal Classification Number: 551.55' 2

ISBN-13: 978 07496 6924 9
ISBN-10: 07496 6924 1

Printed in China

Contents

What is a Hurricane?   4

Where Hurricanes Happen   6

How Hurricanes Happen   8

Anatomy of a Hurricane   10

Predictable Build-up   12

Wild Winds and Water   14

Riding the Storm   16

Human Catastrophe   18

Helping Out   20

Terrible Aftermath   22

Environmental Impact   24

Keeping an Eye on Things   26

Danger Ahead   28

Ten of the Deadliest Hurricanes,
Cyclones and Typhoons   30

Hurricane Names   30

Glossary and Further Information   31

Index   32

What is a Hurricane?

A hurricane is a furious, spiralling tropical storm system that can smash buildings apart and hurl trees, cars and massive chunks of debris far into the air. Wind speeds in a hurricane can reach more than 250 kilometres per hour. The wind brings with it torrential rain and thunderstorms. A hurricane roars in from the ocean and lashes the coast for hours causing terrible damage, but dies down quite quickly as it moves further inland.

▼ Sand whips through a parking lot in Fort Lauderdale, Texas, as Hurricane Katrina (2005) hits the USA.

Angry gods and 'big winds'

Tropical storm systems in the Americas are called hurricanes, but they are known by different names around the world. People in the Americas call them hurricanes after the ancient Mayan and Taino god of wind, storms and destruction, Hurakan or Jurakan. In south-east Asia, where tropical storms come from the Pacific, people call them typhoons, from the Japanese *Tai Foon*, meaning 'great wind'. In India and Australia tropical storms are called cyclones.

A severe tropical storm can be officially classed as a hurricane, typhoon or cyclone if it has winds that blow faster than 118 kilometres per hour.

Hurricanes in history

Hurricanes, cyclones and typhoons have always happened, but because many strike areas where people did not keep written records, we do not have detailed accounts of them going back very far in time. As soon as Europeans began to visit South and Central America, they encountered hurricanes. Christopher Columbus's ship sheltered from a hurricane in a bay in 1502, but 20 other ships were sunk by the storm on their way back to Spain.

▲ *A hurricane and resulting sea flood in Galveston, Texas, USA, in 1900 destroyed the town and killed around 8,000 people.*

CASE STUDY

The Great Hurricane, 1780

Three hurricanes struck the West Indies in 1780, the worst of which killed 22,000 people over eight days, making it the deadliest hurricane ever to strike the western hemisphere. It destroyed nearly every building in Barbados, flattened St Lucia, demolished St Pierre, the capital of Martinique, and on St Vincent it sent a storm surge six metres high that washed villages out to sea. Most of the British fleet at St Lucia was sunk, as well as 15 Dutch ships in Grenada. It would be 200 years before another hurricane would claim more than 10,000 lives in the Atlantic.

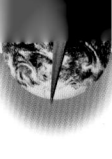

Where Hurricanes Happen

Tropical storms occur in tropical regions of the Atlantic, Indian and Pacific Oceans. The water temperature must be at least 26.5 °C (79.7 °F) for the storm to be able to gather enough strength to be classed as a hurricane. Most Atlantic hurricanes form off the west coast of Africa, then drift westwards to reach land in Central America and the Caribbean.

Landfall

When a hurricane, cyclone or typhoon reaches land, it wreaks destruction along the coast and continues its path inland. After hitting land the storm rapidly loses power as it is no longer heated from beneath by tropical seas. Within 12 hours most of the force has been spent – though it can travel as far as 175 miles inland before dying out.

▼ *The people of Chockwe, Mozambique, depend on rainstorms – but floods are still disruptive.*

Storm zones

The most destructive hurricanes strike the south-eastern coast of the USA, Central America and the Caribbean. Typhoons plague the coasts around the Indian Ocean and many parts of the Pacific Ocean. In the Indian Ocean, they most often strike Indonesia, India, Sri Lanka and Thailand, but also hit Madagascar and east Africa. In the Pacific they are most common around Japan, eastern China and the Philippines, but can also strike the west coast of Australia and New Guinea. Their impact is greatest in areas where most people live.

The Caroline and Marianas island chains and the north coast of Luzon Island in the Philippines have the largest number of tropical storms of anywhere in the world, with around ten each year. Mozambique in Africa depends on the rain brought by tropical storms to boost its water supplies, but the country frequently floods as a result of these typhoons.

▲ *Jupiter's red spot – a giant, ancient storm system.*

GREATEST STORM IN THE SOLAR SYSTEM

The planet Jupiter has a large red spot, which is actually a massive storm system. Like a hurricane, it consists of winds whirling in a circle at great speeds – around 400 kilometres per hour. Jupiter is a gas giant – a planet made entirely of gas – so the storm will never drift over land and die down. The storm has been raging for at least 300 years – it was recorded as soon as the telescope was invented. The storm is 24,800 kilometres across, covering about the same area as the whole of the Earth's surface.

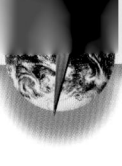

How Hurricanes Happen

A tropical storm builds up over the sea where equatorial winds from different directions meet. The warm air spirals upwards, taking heat and moisture from the sea and growing increasingly strong.

Drawing power from the sea

An Atlantic hurricane begins as a thunderstorm off the west coast of Africa and then becomes a tropical depression. This is a system of swirling clouds and rain, with winds of less than 62 kilometres per hour. Warm air, carrying evaporated water, rises from the surface of the sea. The air cools as it rises, and the water vapour condenses to form rain clouds, which add to the growing storm. Heat escapes from the condensing water and warms the air higher up, which rises in turn, setting up a cycle of warm air being sucked up from the ocean, losing its water to storm clouds and warming more air. The rising column pulls ever more warm air and water from the surface of the sea.

Colliding winds

Winds from different directions collide and circle around the column of rising air and

▼ *A satellite image of Tropical Depression Rita (2005) forming over the Bahamas in the Caribbean.*

moisture, setting up a circular wind pattern. Much higher up, a stronger wind blowing in a single direction carries the warm air away, which in turn pulls up yet more air. High air pressure above the storm helps to suck in more air at the bottom where the air pressure is low. The wind speed increases, first to tropical storm strength (54.7–117.5 kilometres per hour) and finally to hurricane force – 118 kilometres per hour, or above.

◀ *A tornado destroys a house in Texas, USA, in 2004 – a year with a record number of tornadoes.*

TORNADOES

Tornadoes are small, rapidly circling whirlwinds. They may travel ahead of hurricanes, or in their wake (behind them), but they can also occur on their own, inland. A tornado forms beneath a storm cloud, when air is sucked up into the storm cloud from the ground. Sometimes up to two kilometres wide, a tornado can travel at 55 kilometres per hour and have winds of up to 250 kilometres per hour. Rising warm air sucks in more air from beneath the tornado in the same way as happens in a hurricane. A tornado can appear to jump if its vortex (whirling centre) is disturbed – the tornado stops briefly but often reforms in a slightly different place.

Anatomy of a Hurricane

Hurricanes have a very clear structure, and all hurricanes share the same characteristics.

Parts of a hurricane

The destructive part of a hurricane is the whirling band of wind and rainstorms. In the centre of the storm is a still area with very low air pressure called the eye. A thick bank of cloud and rain just around the eye is called the eyewall. The eyewall contains the strongest winds and rains. Outside the eyewall there may be a moat – an area of reduced rain. A thin veil of very high cloud over the top of the hurricane system, made of tiny ice crystals, is called the veil of cirrus. The hurricane can extend 18 kilometres upwards. Widths vary, but a large hurricane can be 480 kilometres wide. Some large typhoons have measured 1300 kilometres across.

Under pressure

A hurricane is a low pressure system. The air at the centre of the storm is at very low pressure – indeed, the lowest air pressures recorded on Earth have been at the eye of a hurricane. Because the air pressure is so low, warm air and water are drawn up into the hurricane, continually feeding it.

▼ *The eyewall of Hurricane Katrina (2005), seen from within the hurricane.*

Saffir-Simpson hurricane scale

The scale used for reporting the size of hurricanes is based on the wind speed. Hurricanes with very strong winds cause terrible damage.

Category	Wind speeds	Damage
1	119–153 kilometres per hour	Little damage to buildings; coastal flooding
2	154–177 kilometres per hour	Damage to roofs, doors and windows; flood damage to piers; some trees blown down
3	178–209 kilometres per hour	Structural damage to small buildings; large trees blown down; coastal and inland flooding; flood damage to small structures
4	210–249 kilometres per hour	Roofs lost from small buildings; serious erosion of beach areas; inland flooding
5	Over 249 kilometres per hour	Roofs lost from all buildings; some buildings destroyed or blown away; serious flood damage to all structures near the coast

▼ *A satellite image of Hurricane Isabel (2003), near Puerto Rico in the Caribbean.*

HURRICANE WINDS

Storms whip around in a hurricane at speeds of 160 to 250 kilometres per hour, or even 320 kilometres per hour in a very severe Pacific typhoon. Hurricane Wilma (2005) had the fastest winds recorded in an Atlantic hurricane at 281 kilometres per hour. The winds in a hurricane circle anticlockwise in the northern hemisphere and clockwise in the southern hemisphere. This is because of the effect of the spinning of the Earth on the movement of the wind and cloud. The movement of the Earth appears anticlockwise in the northern hemisphere and clockwise in the southern hemisphere.

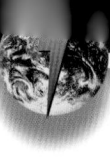

Predictable Build-up

Hurricanes are part of the normal weather patterns that happen around the world each year. In the Atlantic the hurricane season lasts from 1 June to 30 November.

Wind and water

Every year hot and cold winds blow at certain times and in certain places as part of the global weather pattern. There are also regular patterns to the temperatures of the sea in different areas. Hurricanes happen when certain patterns of wind and sea temperature occur at the same time.

Meteorologists (people who study the weather) track wind speeds and study satellite photographs of weather systems to help them spot when a hurricane is brewing. They use computer modelling techniques to predict the likely path of a growing hurricane.

▼ *Violent seas batter the shore in Jamaica as Hurricane Gilbert (1988) makes landfall.*

Helping people to safety

When a hurricane is expected, governments can warn people to take shelter or move to a safe area. Because weather systems are immensely complex and can change quickly, predictions are not always accurate. Scientists can only predict the wind speeds that will occur on land just before the hurricane hits the coast.

Sometimes, it is difficult for governments to decide whether to risk evacuating people needlessly or to leave them where they may be in danger. Evacuation can lead to road traffic accidents, and unnecessary evacuations can make people less likely to take notice of similar warnings in future.

▲ *Traffic blocks the highway as people try to escape the path of Hurricane Floyd in Georgia, USA (1999).*

HURRICANE NAMES

Since 1953, hurricanes have been given human names. There are different sets of names in use around the world. For Atlantic hurricanes, a set of 21 names, each starting with a different letter of the alphabet, is available for use each year. As a hurricane is announced, it is given the next free name. If all the names are used up – if there are more than 21 hurricanes in a year – letters of the Greek alphabet are used as names instead. Six lists of names are used in rotation. If a hurricane is particularly bad, or causes many deaths, its name is retired and replaced by a new name. There is a table of names for hurricanes from 2006–2010 on page 30.

Wild Winds and Water

Although a hurricane causes most damage to people once it hits land, its effects out at sea can be devastating to shipping. When it strikes the coast, the accompanying rain, flooding and raging tides can sometimes cause more damage than the winds themselves.

▼ *Pedestrians in Fort Lauderdale, Florida, USA, struggle to walk through storms caused by Hurricane Katrina (2005).*

Out at sea

All hurricanes start out at sea and some travel thousands of kilometres before reaching land. They can sink large and small boats, and it is difficult to use either rescue boats or helicopters to help shipwrecked sailors during a hurricane.

As a hurricane approaches land, it pushes a huge storm surge – a large wave of water – ahead of it. This floods harbours and beaches and smashes through storm defences.

In the air

Hurricanes would obviously be very dangerous to aircraft, but there is usually enough warning for pilots to keep well away from them. Even so, strong winds hundreds of kilometres from the hurricane itself can cause rough conditions. More importantly, high winds can hamper emergency work, and rescue helicopters and planes carrying relief supplies cannot approach the disaster zone until the winds drop.

Super typhoons

Extra strong typhoons, more powerful than any Atlantic hurricanes, are called super typhoons. With winds well over 240 kilometres per hour and even as much as 320 kilometres per hour, they cause terrible devastation if they hit an inhabited stretch of coast. The largest ever recorded was Super Typhoon Tip, which formed in the north-west Pacific in 1979. It was 2,174 kilometres across and had wind speeds of up to 306 kilometres per hour, but fortunately it did not strike land. Increasingly large and powerful hurricanes, which scientists have called hypercanes, are expected in the Atlantic, too, as global weather conditions change.

▲ *Fishing boats washed ashore in Bayou La Batre, Mississippi, USA, by Hurricane Katrina (2005).*

CASE STUDY

Hakata Bay, 1281

In 1281, a great typhoon destroyed the invasion fleet that the Mongol leader Kublai Kahn had assembled to attack Japan. It ripped through Hakata Bay in south-west Japan, sinking nearly 2,000 of the fleet of 2,200 and drowning between 45,000 and 65,000 troops. An earlier invasion fleet had met the same fate in 1274, with the loss of 13,000 men. The Japanese gave the Hakata Bay typhoon the name Kamikaze, meaning 'divine wind', as it seemed as though God had sent it to save them.

Riding the Storm

The approach of a hurricane is terrifying for the people who live near the coast. Even though hurricanes happen every year, each one usually hits a fairly small strip of coast, so most people do not see many large hurricanes.

On the beach

The storm surge is the first part of the hurricane to strike land. When a storm surge combines with high tide, the effects can be particularly devastating. Waves can be up to 13 metres high, washing over harbours and beachfronts and battering through storm barriers and sea walls. The waves tear boats from their moorings and smash them against harbour walls, or even carry them far inland.

As the wind makes its way over the beach, it whips up the sand into a cloud. Sometimes the sand can become electrically charged in the storm clouds, and glow with static electricity.

▶ *Shop workers board up windows in advance of Hurricane Fran (1996) in North Carolina, USA.*

Violent winds

The winds grow in strength, often bringing torrential rain at the same time. Winds are so strong that they tear up trees, pull the roofs off houses and even hurl vehicles and small buildings around. Houses sometimes explode, as the pressure inside them is much higher than the pressure outside. People may be blown over, smashed into objects or picked up by the wind and carried some distance before they are dropped.

After a while the wind calms and many people think the danger is over. But this is the eye of the hurricane passing, and the storm soon restarts as violently as before. People who come out from shelter when the eye passes over them are often caught unawares by the second wind.

▲ *A house damaged by Hurricane Hugo (1989) in South Carolina, USA.*

CASE STUDY

Hurricane Mitch, 1998

Hurricane Mitch ripped through Nicaragua in 1998. It first hit land as a tropical storm in Florida but gathered strength as it passed over the sea again. Torrential rains caused flooding and mudslides, killing 11,000 people and making it the most deadly hurricane since the Great Hurricane of 1780. The flooding was made worse by the slow movement of the hurricane over land – it moved at 7 kilometres per hour, which gave plenty of time for rain to fall.

Human Catastrophe

▼ *New Orleans, USA, as it was before Hurricane Katrina (2005) and then 17 days afterwards, with much of the city flooded.*

Many people fear the winds of a hurricane, but most deaths are caused by flooding and the after-effects of the storm.

Immediate dangers

People caught in a hurricane may be whisked up into the air and smashed against trees or buildings, or collide with other objects carried by the wind. They may be trapped in falling buildings, hit by debris carried by the wind, or injured by glass and masonry falling from high-rise buildings.

Hurricanes are often accompanied by floods from the sea, from rivers bursting their banks and from torrential rain. Often, more people drown in floods than are killed by the winds. In some areas, floods can lead to deadly mudslides and landslides that bury people alive.

After the storm

Even when the winds die down, the danger is not over. The land may stay flooded for weeks. People may have nowhere to shelter from continuing bad weather and no food or clean water. Injured and sick people are often cut off from medical help. Survivors may begin to suffer from exposure if the weather is cold; or they may suffer dehydration, sunstroke or heat exhaustion if it is hot. In some areas they may be prey to poisonous snakes, dangerous animals and disease-carrying insects.

In refugee camps and emergency accommodation, people are often crowded together in unsanitary conditions without adequate food, water or medical attention. Disease spreads rapidly in such conditions. After a cyclone in Bangladesh in 1876, which killed 100,000 people, a further 100,000 died in the cholera epidemic that followed it.

▲ *A couple and their baby escape from their car in the New Orleans floods brought by Hurricane Katrina (2005).*

CASE STUDY

Galveston, 1900

The hurricane that hit the island of Galveston, Texas, in September 1900 caused the worst natural disaster in US history. With winds of up to 225 kilometres per hour and a storm surge of 4.8 metres, it killed more than 6,000 people and destroyed 3,600 buildings. With no early warning systems or tracking technology, the people of Galveston did not know the hurricane was coming and were not evacuated. The destruction was so severe and the conditions so bad that the dead were piled up and burnt where they lay.

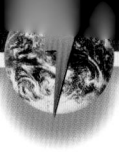

Helping Out

When a hurricane strikes an inhabited area, help of many kinds is needed immediately. Often, local emergency services cannot cope with the demand and national and sometimes international aid from governments and charities is needed.

Immediate tasks

The most urgent work for rescue groups and emergency services is to free people who are trapped or who are cut off by flood waters, and to move injured people to safety. Even minor injuries can be fatal as wading through sewage and mud can cause wounds to become infected. Whether they are injured or not, survivors need emergency housing, medical supplies, food and water.

▼ *Refugees from Hurricane Katrina (2005) pack the Astrodome sports stadium in Houston, Texas, USA.*

It is important to remove dead bodies from the disaster zone, too, as their presence is not only upsetting for survivors but soon leads to disease. Bodies decaying in water that provides drinking supplies can cause outbreaks of gastroenteritis, which may be deadly when treatment and clean water are not available.

Cut off

It can be very difficult for help to reach the

disaster area. Even without flooding, debris can block or destroy roads, railways and ports, making it impossible for people to move out of the area or for help to reach them. Landslides or mudslides may destroy key bridges and roads. If strong winds and rain continue after the hurricane, planes and helicopters may not be usable.

Leaving the area

Even after the hurricane, it may be necessary to evacuate the area if it is flooded or if further bad weather is expected. If communication networks, road and rail links have been damaged – or if they never existed – it can be very difficult to move people to safety.

▲ *Rescuers save a baby from raging flood waters near Guayama in the Caribbean after Hurricane Hortense (1996).*

CASE STUDY

Hurricane Katrina, 2005

Hurricane Katrina struck New Orleans on the coast of the USA in August 2005. It broke the levees (walls that hold back the lake and river behind the city) and the city was flooded to depths of six metres. Thousands of people were encouraged to make their way to sports stadiums and conference centres for temporary shelter. But these centres lacked electricity, sanitation, air conditioning and sufficient food and water. Conditions soon deteriorated, with people living in filth and falling ill. Local and federal government were heavily criticized for their handling of the disaster.

Terrible Aftermath

In the days and weeks following a hurricane, the extent of the damage to people's lives as well as to property slowly emerges. Whole families may have been killed, communities destroyed, and people's lives changed for ever.

Cleaning up

As soon as a hurricane is over, local, national and international teams start rebuilding road and rail links so that emergency workers can reach people who are trapped or stranded. They may need to clear debris, drain or pump out flood water and rebuild sea walls or levees to protect the area from further damage by other hurricanes and winds. They also need to demolish unsafe buildings and clear the land.

▼ *A settlement in Bangladesh devastated by a cyclone in 1991.*

Devastated communities

Many people lose not only their homes but family members and friends when a catastrophic hurricane strikes. For them, life will never be the same again. When many people have suffered the same fate, it may seem as though the community itself can never be rebuilt. In addition, the area may be left without essential amenities such as water, electricity, schools, hospitals, shops and transport systems. These can take years to rebuild.

Rebuilding

Often, people want to remain in the area where they have always lived, even if there is a danger of further hurricanes at some time in the future. Planners and engineers can design buildings that will be safer in the face of future storms, but making storm-proof buildings can be very expensive. Many areas prone to hurricanes are very poor and under-developed and people cannot afford the necessary precautions. Their rebuilt houses remain vulnerable to future storms.

▲ *A man clears up after a fire started by Hurricane Claudette (2003) wrecked his beach house in Texas, USA.*

CASE STUDY

Bangladesh, 1970

In November 1970, the worst cyclone disaster of the twentieth century struck East Pakistan (now Bangladesh), a low-lying coastal country north-east of India. Between 300,000 and 500,000 people were killed. Winds of up to 190 kilometres per hour lashed the coast, destroying the flimsy housing of the poor, causing the river Ganges to flood and swamping essential farmland. Bangladesh is an area often hit by cyclones. Although some housing is built in a protected area, the poorest people cannot afford to live there. However, there are now over 1,600 cyclone shelters in Bangladesh that one million people can use.

Environmental Impact

The impact on human lives and homes is the first concern of relief agencies and governments in the aftermath of a hurricane. Yet the impact on the environment usually affects people, too. For many people, particularly in undeveloped and poor areas, the farmland, forests and seas provide food or a livelihood.

Forests and farms

A hurricane can rip the trees and other vegetation from the land, destroying orchards and forests that have been growing for decades or centuries. Hurricanes can also cause flooding from the sea or from rainstorms or from rivers bursting their banks. In a flood, farmland and forests can be damaged by salt water or sewage. Crops may not grow and farm animals or wild animals may die. For local people who live by farming or hunting, this disaster can lead to famine or economic collapse.

Flooding can also wash the topsoil from the land into rivers, making the land less fertile and the rivers shallower. A shallow river is more likely to burst its banks and flood the land again.

▼ *Beech trees destroyed by hurricane-force winds in Kent, England, in 1987.*

Pollution

A hurricane can tear down factories and oil refineries, drive ships onto the rocks so that they spill their cargoes, and hurl all kinds of debris across the land and sea. Oil escaping from damaged oil wells, refineries or tanks, or chemicals from industrial plants may contaminate both land and sea with disastrous effects on wildlife. If a local community relies on fishing, this kind of environmental damage can be disastrous. Areas dependent on tourism for their income need to clean up very quickly to avoid an economic crisis.

◄ *A boy in Bangladesh helps his goat to safety through flood waters in 2004.*

CORAL REEFS IN DANGER

In Samoa and other Pacific islands, coral reefs are often damaged by typhoons. The large waves whipped up by a typhoon batter the reef, breaking off chunks that may have taken centuries to grow. The sea carries broken lumps of coral into island lagoons where they crash into inland reefs. Topsoil washed from islands into the sea cuts off sunlight to the reef, preventing plant growth. The nutrients in the soil encourage algae to grow in the sea, further disturbing the fragile balance of the reef.

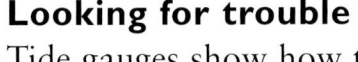

Keeping an Eye on Things

Meteorologists monitor sea and wind conditions around the world to help provide early warning of coming tropical storms. Even with the best computer modelling systems, though, the predictions meteorologists can make about tropical storms are not perfect.

Looking for trouble

Tide gauges show how the swell in the ocean grows as a storm is brewing. Wind gauges measure the speed of the wind, though sometimes a hurricane, cyclone or typhoon is so powerful it destroys the gauges that are measuring it. Pictures beamed from satellites circling above the Earth reveal the movement and patterns of storm clouds that may build into a hurricane or typhoon. Information gathered from these instruments can be compared with data from previous hurricanes to help meteorologists predict whether a hurricane is building, where it will go and how powerful it may be when it makes landfall.

Efficient tracking of hurricanes with satellites only began in about 1960. Before then, many tropical storms went unrecorded if they did not hit populated areas. Most of what we know about hurricanes in the past is derived from ships' logs.

Being prepared

In some areas prone to tropical storms, people prepare for the worst. In Australia and the Bahamas, many people have storm shutters fitted to their houses. Some have shelters – specially built strong rooms – where they can hide during the worst storms. Hurricane drills are practice sessions in which people take refuge as though a tropical storm were on its way. Drills help to make sure everyone knows where to go and can take action to protect themselves if a storm really does arrive.

▲ *A hurricane hunter flies into Hurricane Ophelia (2005).*

HURRICANE HUNTERS

Hurricane hunters are planes that deliberately chase hurricanes, flying as close as possible and even trying to get into the eye of the hurricane and fly with it. They can fly at heights of up to 12 kilometres. Hurricane hunters carry wind gauges called anemometers, used to measure the speed of the wind, and radars to measure the amount of rain. The planes can also drop instruments attached to parachutes that measure wind conditions and transmit their readings along with their own location as they fall. New robotic planes that fly without a pilot or crew will be able to carry out even more dangerous hurricane reconnaissance work.

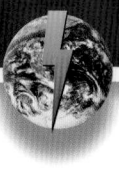

Danger Ahead

▲ *A huge rebuilding programme is needed to restore New Orleans following Hurricane Katrina (2005).*

Hurricanes have become stronger since the 1990s, and there may be more of them. Some scientists suggest that they may become even more frequent and damaging in the future.

Hot seas

To form, a hurricane needs a warm sea beneath colliding winds. Many scientists believe that the seas are becoming warmer as global warming takes effect. Global warming is a rise in temperature across the whole of the planet, probably caused by people burning large quantities of fossil fuels (coal, oil and gas) for energy. As we burn fossil fuels, the gas carbon dioxide is released. This builds up in the top layer of the atmosphere and acts like a blanket, stopping heat escaping from the Earth and making the planet warmer. If the seas are warmer, the conditions needed for hurricanes to form will occur more often. The number of category 4 or 5 hurricanes doubled between 1970 and 2005. Over that time the top 300 metres of the sea warmed by 0.5 °C.

More floods

As the temperature on Earth rises, ice at the north and south poles melts and pours into the sea, raising the level of the sea. Coastal areas may flood, and during a hurricane it will take less water to flood further inland.

The effects of hurricanes will be more damaging as flooding will happen more easily. Areas outside current hurricane zones may be subject to floods, too, as sea levels rise. Storm barriers built for current sea levels may offer little help.

Rising temperatures also cause more rain to fall with hurricanes, and that increases flooding, too. The rainfall that came with Hurricane Katrina in 2005 was, scientists estimate, 7 per cent higher than it would have been without global warming.

OUTSIDE THE ZONE

In 2004, the first hurricane ever recorded in the South Atlantic rang warning bells for scientists. It was unofficially named Catarina as it struck land in Santa Catarina, Brazil – there is no naming system for hurricanes in the South Atlantic as they have not happened before. Scientists cannot tell yet whether hurricanes in the South Atlantic will become more common, or whether it was a one-off event.

▲ *A colour-coded map based on satellite images shows the variation in sea temperature around the globe.*

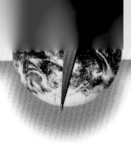

TEN OF THE DEADLIEST HURRICANES, CYCLONES AND TYPHOONS

WHEN	WHERE	CASUALTIES
1970	Bangladesh	300,000–500,000
1881	Haiphong, Vietnam	300,000
1737	Calcutta, India	Up to 300,000
1876	Bay of Bengal	200,000
1991	Bangladesh	138,000
1882	Mumbai, India	100,000
1864	Calcutta, India	70,000
1281	Hakata Bay, Japan	45,000–65,000
1780	Martinique, St Eustatius and Barbados (Great Hurricane)	22,000
1998	Nicaragua and Honduras (Hurricane Mitch)	11,000

HURRICANE NAMES

The following names have been allocated to hurricanes in the North Atlantic for the years 2006–2010.

2006	2007	2008	2009	2010
Alberto	Andrea	Arthur	Ana	Alex
Beryl	Barry	Bertha	Bill	Bonnie
Chris	Chantal	Cristobal	Claudette	Colin
Debby	Dean	Dolly	Danny	Danielle
Ernesto	Erin	Edouard	Erika	Earl
Florence	Felix	Fay	Fred	Fiona
Gordon	Gabrielle	Gustav	Grace	Gaston
Helene	Humberto	Hanna	Henri	Hermine
Isaac	Ingrid	Ike	Ida	Igor
Joyce	Jerry	Josephine	Joaquin	Julia
Kirk	Karen	Kyle	Kate	Karl
Leslie	Lorenzo	Laura	Larry	Lisa
Michael	Melissa	Marco	Mindy	Matthew
Nadine	Noel	Nana	Nicholas	Nicole
Oscar	Olga	Omar	Odette	Otto
Patty	Pablo	Paloma	Peter	Paula
Rafael	Rebekah	Rene	Rose	Richard
Sandy	Sebastien	Sally	Sam	Shary
Tony	Tanya	Teddy	Teresa	Tomas
Valerie	Van	Vicky	Victor	Virginie
William	Wendy	Wilfred	Wanda	Walter

GLOSSARY

cholera A disease that causes very bad diarrhoea, sickness and cramps and often leads to death.

condense Make droplets of liquid from a vapour (gas) by cooling.

debris Rubbish and broken items.

equatorial winds Warm winds around the equator that follow established patterns.

evacuate Leave an area because of danger.

evaporate Change from a liquid to a gas.

eye The central, calm area of a hurricane.

eyewall The band of thick cloud around the eye of a hurricane.

hemisphere One half of the world.

meteorologist A person who studies the weather.

reconnaissance The exploration or examination of an area to gather information about it.

satellite An object that orbits (travels around) a planet.

topsoil The layer of soil rich in nutrients in which plants grow.

tornado A small, fierce, whirling wind system.

torrential Very severe.

tropical Relating to the tropics – the areas just above and below the equator.

vapour Gas.

vortex A spiralling system, like a whirlwind.

wind gauge An instrument used to measure the speed of the wind.

FURTHER INFORMATION

Books

Extreme Weather: A Guide and Record Book by Christopher Burt (Norton, 2004)

Eyewitness Guide: Hurricane and Tornado by Jack Challoner (Dorling Kindersley, 2004)

Horrible Geography: Stormy Weather by Anita Ganeri (Scholastic, 1999)

Magic Treehouse Research Guides: Twisters and Other Terrible Storms by Will Osborne (Random House, 2003)

Websites

http://www.bbc.co.uk/science/hottopics/naturaldisasters/hurricanes.shtml

http://www.hurricaneville.com/historic.html

http://observe.arc.nasa.gov/nasa/earth/hurricane/splash.html

http://kids.earth.nasa.gov/archive/hurricane/index.html

Videos/DVDs

Key Largo directed by John Huston (Warner Brothers, 1948)

The Day After Tomorrow directed by Roland Emmerich (20th Century Fox, 2004)

The Hurricane directed by John Ford (Samuel Goldwyn Studios, 1937)

Twister directed by Jan de Bont (Warner Home Video, 1996)

INDEX

Page numbers in **bold** refer to illustrations.

Africa 6, 7, 8
aid 20
Atlantic Ocean 5, 6, 8, 11, 12, 13, 15, 29
Australia 4, 7, 27

Bangladesh 19, **22**, 23, **25**, 30
Brazil 29

Caribbean 6, **8**, 11, **12**, **21**, 27, 30
Central America 5, 6, 17, 30
China 7
clouds 8, 9, 10, 11, 16, 26
cyclones 4, 19, **22**, 23

death 19, 20, 22, 23
destruction 4, 5, **5**, 6, 11, 14, 16, 17, 18, 19, 21, 22
disease 18, 19, 20

emergency relief 14, 18–19, 20, 22, 24
environmental damage 24–5
erosion 11
evacuation 12–13, **13**, 19, 21, 31
eye 10, 17, 27, 31
eyewall 10, **10**, 31

flooding **5**, 7, 11, 14, 17, 18, **18**, **19**, 20, 21, 22, 23, 24, **25**, 28–9

global warming 28

hurricane drills 27
hurricane hunters 27, **27**
hurricane names 13, 30
hurricanes
Claudette (2003) **23**
Dora (2005) **26**
Floyd (1999) **13**
Fran (1996) **16**
Galveston, Texas (1900) **5**, 19
Gilbert (1988) **12**

Great Hurricane (1780) 5, 17, 30
Hortense (1996) **21**
Hugo (1989) **17**
Isabel (2003) **11**
Katrina (2005) **4**, **10**, **14**, 15, 18, **19**, 20, 21, **28**, 29
Mitch (1998) 17, 30
Ophelia (2005) **27**
Wilma (2005) 11
hurricane warnings 12
hypercanes 15

India 4, 6, 23, 30
Indian Ocean 6
Indonesia 6
injury 18, 20

Japan 7, 30
Jupiter's red spot 7, **7**

landslides 18, 21

meteorology 12, 26, 31
Mozambique **6**, 7

New Guinea 7

Pacific Ocean 4, 6, 11, 15
Philippines 7
pollution 25

rain 4, **6**, 7, 8, 10, 14, 17, 21, 24, 27, 29
rebuilding 22, 23, **28**
refugees 18, **20**
rescue 14, 20

Saffir-Simpson scale 11
shelters 17, 23, 27
South America 5
Sri Lanka 6
storm surges 14, 16, 19

super typhoons 15
Tip (1979) 15

Thailand 6
thunderstorms 4, 8
tornadoes 9, **9**, 31
tropical depressions 8
Rita (2005) 8
tropical storms 4, 6, 7, 8, 9, 26
typhoons 4, 6, 10, 25
Hakata Bay (1281) 15

USA **4**, 5, 6, **9**, 13, **14**, **15**, **16**, 17, **17**, **18**, 19, **19**, **20**, 21, **23**, **28**

West Indies 5
winds 4, 8, 9, 10, 11, 12, 14, 15, 16, 17, 18, 19, 21, 22, 27, 28, 31